RUSH LIMBAUGH IN NIGHT SCHOOL

BY CHARLIE VARON

★

★

DRAMATISTS
PLAY SERVICE
INC.

This play is dedicated to Marc Fisher,
friend, fellow prankster and radio head

RUSH LIMBAUGH IN NIGHT SCHOOL was produced by Woolly Mammoth Theatre Company (Howard Shalwitz, Artistic Director) in Washington, D.C., on November 8, 1995. The design coordinator was Daniel Schrader; the production manager was Rick Fiori; and the production stage manager was Cheryl Repeta. All roles were played by Charlie Varon.

RUSH LIMBAUGH IN NIGHT SCHOOL was produced by Second Stage Theatre (Carole Rothman, Artistic Director; Suzanne Schwartz Davidson, Producing Director) in New York City, in March, 1995. It was directed by David Ford; the set design was by Sherri Adler; the lighting design was by Donald Holder; and the production stage manager was Elaine Bayless. All roles were played by Charlie Varon.

RUSH LIMBAUGH IN NIGHT SCHOOL received its premiere at The Marsh (Stephanie Weisman, Artistic Director) in San Francisco, California, on October 7, 1994. It was directed by Martin Higgins; the lighting design was by Chris French. All roles were played by Charlie Varon.

ACKNOWLEDGMENTS

Developed with David Ford

Original production directed by Martin Higgins

Developed in association with The Marsh, Stephanie Weisman, artistic director

Additional Script Collaboration: Martin Higgins, Josh Kornbluth, Myra Levy, Jim Rosenau, Leonard Pitt, Ellen Sebastian, Bob Gavrich.

Special thanks to Philip Armour, Carla Befera, Sam Blazer, Peter Buchanan, Valerie Gilbert, Howie Gordon, Jonathan Karpf and Kathie Zaretsky, Barbara Levy, Scoop Nisker, Marilyn Pittman, Scott Rosenberg, Joel Schechter, Zipporah and Maurice Varon, Claude Whitmyer and The Zellerbach Family Fund.

AUTHOR'S NOTE

I wrote this play as a piece of topical political satire with myself as the only performer. Now, contemplating the possibility that others will mount productions of the play, I foresee certain questions that a director will face:

TIME

It was 1994 when I wrote *Rush Limbaugh in Night School.* I set the play in the spring of 1996 — which was then the near future and is now the receding past. If you're contemplating a production of this play, you must somehow deal with this question of time. I can think of two ways to do this:

1. Leave as is all dates and references to time. Put a note in the program to the effect that the play was written in 1994 as a fantasy and in no way purports to document actual events.
2. Change the dates to a year still in the future — e.g., a production in the year 1999 might set the play in 2002. Update or delete, as necessary, references to prominent people. For instance, the 1996 Presidential election material would have to be altered or cut. (As I write this in 1996, I wonder whether Rush Limbaugh will even be on the air in three or five or ten years.)

SOLO SHOW OR MULTIPLE ACTORS?

This play was written for one performer and, though I'm sure it can be performed by a larger cast, I cannot imagine the changes necessary to pull that off. However large or small the company, do feel free to experiment and adapt the text to your needs.

LIMBAUGH ON THE AIR

Several scenes feature Rush Limbaugh on the air. Here the script is an approximation of my performance, which itself was an impression of Limbaugh's rambling, improvisatory and highly mannered style. It is hard to render on the page all of his broadcast tics: the stopping-and-starting, the self-interrupting, the changes in pitch and pace that are the equivalent of italic type, raised eyebrows, etc. Not to mention the occasional grunts, groans, snapping of paper, and rapping of knuckles on a wooden surface. The actor playing Limbaugh should feel less accountable to the task of speaking the exact text than to conveying the general meaning of the words and the quality of Limbaugh's on-air persona. Take liberties!

Over the course of productions in several cities, I have performed the play both with and without microphone amplification for Limbaugh's radio scenes. Experiment.

There is also the matter of the sound engineer whom Limbaugh addresses several times in the play. In the script this person is named Chris — after my San Francisco sound and lighting operator, Chris French — but feel free to use the name of someone in the booth at your production. Hand signals from Limbaugh to the engineer are also a fun bit of business.

THE PLEDGE BREAK

At the end of Act One there is a public television pledge break. It begins with the sound of telephones ringing (you'll need an audio tape of that sound) and continues with a plea for contributions from viewers. Use the call letters of your local public TV station in place of KQED, and feel free to use the names of current programs.

SET, COSTUMES AND PROPS

These will all need to be considered afresh. The play was conceived with a minimal set in mind, a neutral costume for the single actor, and very few props (e.g., no telephone; the actor simply picking up an imaginary phone). It *is* essential to get fresh, ripe pears with long, sturdy stems.

Charlie Varon
June 1996

CHARACTERS

in order of appearance

BOOTH PERCY, political pundit
BARRY GRANATOUR, Rush Limbaugh's manager
NINA EGGLY, a masseuse
NARRATOR
ANNOUNCER
RUSH LIMBAUGH
RAY PARNASSUS, author
BARBARA ITCOTLELIAN, Spanish student, middle-aged
DANIEL HOROWITZ, Spanish student,
in his sixties or seventies
LUIS COLÓN, Spanish student, in his twenties
DR. KARL BRAUTERFELD
DR. ALVIN VOLT
SPALDING GRAY
GARRISON KEILLOR
JACKIE MASON
ELEA AVÓN
J. NEIL RODRIGUEZ
ARNOLD PLEDGE
BBC NEWSCASTER
CABDRIVER
DELBERT BROOK
DR. GINTA ROSH
COKIE ROBERTS
HOMO LUDENS
FBI AGENT

RUSH LIMBAUGH IN NIGHT SCHOOL

ACT ONE

BOOTH PERCY. *(Retrospect interview.)* I don't think anybody can deny what Rush Limbaugh did in terms of redefining the medium of talk radio. *(Interview spotlight fades out. A second interview spotlight fades up.)*
BARRY GRANATOUR. *(Retrospect interview.)* What happened to Rush Limbaugh was very unfortunate. *(Interview spotlight fades out. A third interview spotlight fades up.)*
NINA EGGLY. *(Retrospect interview.)* In spite of everything that was wrong with it, it was still one of the best relationships I've ever had. *(Interview spotlight fades out. Then general lighting for Narrator, C.)*
NARRATOR. Back in 1996, Rush Limbaugh was riding high. His daily radio audience was at its peak, and his income was more than $55 million a year. Now, as he sits in Federal prison, he wonders what went wrong. I'm Rogers Johnson, and *this* is the story of the fall of Rush Limbaugh.
ANNOUNCER. *("Sings" PBS-style introductory music; then:)* Broadcast of this *Frontline* documentary is made possible by *(Does brief audio "sting" or "sound button" while twirling a sign such as the "Viacom" sign — a parody of a public TV funding credit.)* Viacom, a diversified Fortune 500 company mourning the demise of the information superhighway.
NARRATOR. It was an unlikely sequence of events that

brought down Rush Limbaugh. Our story begins on May 27, 1996. That night, Rush Limbaugh was taken out to a celebration dinner at Ben Benson's Steakhouse in New York City. As the waiters served coffee, Rush Limbaugh's manager, Barry Granatour, addressed the guests.

BARRY. *(Tapping a spoon on a glass.)* Ladies and gennimin, thank you, thank you, thank you for coming out to celebrate this extraordinary news. Late this morning, ladies and gennimin, I received the following fax:

(Reads.) "Mr. Barry Granatour, Granatour Management Associates; Dear Mr. Granatour: Based on an independent review of the Arbitron radio ratings survey, we certify that the Rush Limbaugh Program's daily radio audience has now surpassed 60 million listeners."

Don't applaud yet!

Sixty million listeners *means* that every day one out of every hundred people is listening to Rush Limbaugh. On this *planet.* On this *planet.*

N'kay. Sixty million people is more people than have ever seen any play by William Shakespeare — and that includes the plays where authorship is unclear.

And Rush — I promised Rush he would not have to say anything tonight, end of a long week, 22 hours on the air, says he's all talked out — but have any of us ever known Rush *not* to have something to say? Rush, come on up. *(Leads audience in applause.)*

RUSH LIMBAUGH. Ladies and gentlemen, what this man has done. Thirty-six world class filet mignons, flown in this morning from Buenos Aires. How big were those steaks we just ate? Five pounds each! Thirty-six goblets of ice cream: my favorite flavor, macadamia nut.

Barry, what I really want to know is how you got Loren Gazzivich here tonight.

Loren Gazzivich, for those of you who do not know, a writer for The Washington *Post.* Seven and a half years ago, this gentleman wrote an article about me. *(Pulls newspaper clipping out of pocket and rattles it.)* You don't mind if I—? "Limbaugh is a right-wing blabbermouth, and the Limbaugh Phenomenon will soon fizzle." Mr. Gazzivich, a copy of this article was finely diced and blended into your ice cream. Sir, you just ate your words!

NARRATOR. The following morning Rush Limbaugh gets up as usual at 4:00 A.M. and begins his daily routine: scanning his faxes, e-mail messages, and seven morning newspapers; shaving. In the shower Limbaugh watches video highlights of the previous evening's *Nightline, Charlie Rose* and *Dan Quayle* programs.

6:22 A.M.: A stretch limousine pulls up outside 1 Rockefeller Center, and Rush Limbaugh steps out. He is immediately surrounded by two dozen private security guards. Beyond the guards, there is an outer ring of some 80 people wearing blue-and-orange armbands and pressing in with cameras and video recorders. These are fans of Mr. Limbaugh who for $250 each have purchased day passes allowing them to be part of Mr. Limbaugh's Entourage. Now, catching sight of the celebrity, they begin chanting in unison: "Limbaugh! Limbaugh! Limbaugh! Limbaugh!"

Smiling, waving, Mr. Limbaugh leaves the crowd behind and enters the building.

BARRY. Have a seat, Rush. You wanna cuppa coffee? Sit. Take a look at *these.* They're from Fred. *(Hands Rush a piece of paper.)*

RUSH. What is this? My numbers, my audience curve plotted against that of Dick Cavett at the same GRC point in his career. "While Limbaugh's share has continued to increase, the pace of increase itself has slowed. When the numbers are fed into the Microsoft audience projection software, they produce *disturbingly Cavett-like results.* Rodriguez, by contrast, is showing the kind of meteoric gain that Limbaugh showed in 1990 and 1991."

BARRY. Fred thinks you've got six to eight weeks. Then? Cancellation.

RUSH. Barry! This does not make any sense. I'm at 60 million! Rodriguez is only—

BARRY. Rush, four years ago, my wife was having an affair. N'kay, and the investigators I hired to see what she and this Donald were doing — the videotapes they brought back showed that every time the two of them got together, they were doing something different. One time they made love with a lot of asparagus. Another time they got — not the Guarneri Quartet, but one of the major string quartets, to play Vivaldi while they made love on the living room rug.

(Stands.) Rush, my point is not the affair! My point is that they, like the American public, have an insatiable desire for novelty. *(Sits.)* And Rodriguez is — *new.*

RUSH. Six to eight weeks?? Barry, do something! Get me *out* of this!

BARRY. N'kay, let's let's let's keep our heads about us. I've been through this before. What did we do with Henry Winkler? It didn't work.

Rush, like it or not, we are now in the ring with Rodriguez. *(Pause.)*

Have you ever thought about learning Spanish?

Yeah, Spanish! — beat Rodriguez at his own game. Rush, you think you can you learn enough Spanish in four weeks to go on the air bilingual?

NARRATOR. That day Barry Granatour enrolled Rush Limbaugh in an intensive Spanish class at the New School for Social Research, a politically progressive adult-education center in Greenwich Village. He chose the New School because he thought no one there would recognize Mr. Limbaugh. Still, as a precaution, he enrolled him under the name "Russell Lindbergh."

Three years later, the question remains: Why did Rush Limbaugh fail to question the computer projections that forecast his demise? Psychologist Ray Parnassus.

RAY PARNASSUS. *(Interview.)* As I point out in my book *The Half Life of a Celebrity,* the American celebrity lives in a state of perpetual terror, much like a chicken inching its way forward on the slaughterhouse conveyor belt.

NARRATOR. **May 29, 1996.** Barry Granatour applies spirit gum to Rush Limbaugh's upper lip and chin, and pastes on a false mustache and goatee beard. Then he hands Limbaugh a bag of clothes. Limbaugh puts on blue jeans, Birkenstock sandals and a T-shirt bearing the logo of Ben & Jerry's Ice Cream. Barry Granatour recalls what happened.

BARRY. *(Retrospect interview.)* Rush showed absolutely no hesitation in putting on those clothes. He was like a seven year old with a new Halloween costume. He was happy.

NARRATOR. That evening, Spanish class at the New School.

BARBARA ITCOTLELIAN. My name is Barbara Itcotlelian. I'm taking the class because I'm the new executive director of Shopping for Change, we're a nonprofit, socially-responsible cable shopping channel.

DANIEL HOROWITZ. My name is Daniel Horowitz. I was on one of the first Venceremos Brigades to Coova, back in the '60s.

LUIS COLÓN. Okay. My name is Luis Colón. I'm with the Mayor's Advisory Task Force on Youth. I'm Puerto Rican, born and raised in the Bronx, but I never learned Spanish.

RUSH. *Me llamo* Russell Lindbergh, no relation to Charles incidentally, never been kidnapped. Taking the class purely for pleasure.

NARRATOR. The last of the 10 students to introduce herself was a middle-aged woman. Rush Limbaugh immediately noticed that like him, she was wearing a Ben & Jerry's T-shirt. And then he saw her face: Dangling from her ears, two gigantic ice-cream cone earrings, and in between, a mischievous smile framed by small dimples in the cheeks. Rush Limbaugh felt his heart pound in his chest.

NINA. I'm Nina Eggly. For the past 21 years I lived in Santa Fe. And then last year my marriage ended — which incidentally if any of you are thinking of leaving your spouse, was the best thing that's ever happened to me. Anyway, I've made a commitment to myself to be fluent in Spanish by my 50th birthday. I'm 48½ now. I should also say that I do massage, and I'm still building up my practice here in the Village, so if you know anybody who's looking for massage, I'm available.
NARRATOR. What Nina Eggly did *not* say was that that was not her real name. Born Jean Brook, she had grown up the daughter of a wealthy New England industrialist. Then, in college, she joined the militant, left-wing Weather Underground.

Though she was not involved in any of the Weather Underground's violent acts, Jean Brook did manage to incur the wrath of the Federal Government. In 1969, in an act of puckish pranksterism, Jean Brook produced and distributed an FBI-style WANTED poster showing FBI Chief J. Edgar Hoover wearing a pink chiffon gown. She unwittingly touched a nerve in the FBI director, who immediately placed her at the top of the FBI's Most Wanted List, where she remained even after Hoover's death.

After Spanish class, Rush Limbaugh lingered outside the classroom, thinking that when Nina Eggly emerged, he might ask her to join him for an ice cream cone and some Spanish conversation. But when she finally did come out, she was moving briskly. Rush Limbaugh tried to speak, but no words came out of his mouth.
RUSH. Ww — uh —
NARRATOR. Rush Limbaugh then followed Nina Eggly up two flights of stairs to a crowded lecture hall. The room was filled with more than a hundred students, most of them wearing Ben & Jerry's T-shirts. By the time he had found a seat, next to a tall man with a pencil mustache and dark glasses, Rush Limbaugh had lost sight of Nina Eggly. He resigned himself to staying through the class, whatever it turned out to be,

in the hope of catching another glimpse of Nina Eggly.

DR. KARL BRAUTERFELD. Good evening! Welcome! I don't want to get into all the registration rigmarole right now, if you have any questions, please see my assistant Donald, Donald please raise your hand. Thank you, Donald.

First a word about the *title* of this seminar: "Millennial Musings: Reconstructing Meaning in the Age of Letterman and Limbaugh." Is there anyone here tonight who is *not* familiar with David Letterman? All right, we all know who *that* is. How about Rush Limbaugh? Anyone who has *not* heard of Rush Limbaugh? I see one hand.

NARRATOR. The one hand that went up was that of Nina Eggly. Rush Limbaugh's heart skipped a beat when he saw her again.

DR. KARL BRAUTERFELD. By that title I do not mean in any way to disparage the work of either Letterman or Limbaugh. They are both very intelligent, very creative, and they are part of an important industry: The American Cleverness Industry — whose aim is to take from our culture, our society, our communal life such as it is, elements of our shared existence and turn them into nuggets of amusement which will take the place in our consciousness where meaning should be.

Well. I'm going to shut up and turn it over to tonight's guest lecturer, Dr. Alvin Volt.

NARRATOR. During the lecture that followed, Rush Limbaugh's attention was divided between the speaker at the front of the room and Nina Eggly. He noticed that when Nina laughed, her ice cream cone earrings shook back and forth and small dimples formed once again in her cheeks.

ALVIN VOLT. I am holding in my hand a pear. Can all of you see that what I am holding in my hand is a pear? It's an ordinary pear, stem on top, you know there are seeds inside: you think nothing of it.

Because as an urban dweller, you forget that this pear actually came from someplace. You see, this pear was once hanging from the branch of a pear tree. And then someone came along and plucked the pear from the branch of that pear tree.

But you — as you look at this pear, why it looks like something to eat, doesn't it? Snack perhaps, or perhaps dessert. *(He takes out a pocket knife.)* And so you take a cutting implement and you proceed to carve open the pear. *(He does so, and hands pieces of pear to audience members. If someone begins eating, he says, "And already he's eating it. That's all right, don't wait for me.")* Go ahead, take a morsel of the pear, put it into your mouth. *(He puts a piece in his own mouth.)* And what happens? Your molars clamp down on the pear flesh, extrude pear juice, pear pulp. The pear juice and the pear pulp travel up your tongue, sending a message to the tastebuds on your tongue, which those tastebuds in turn relay to the receptors in your brain, which tell you that what you're eating is ... *(Looks to audience for answer; someone says, "A pear.")* Yes, a pear! It's not an apple. It's not a nectarine. It's not fried rice. It is, as he so aptly put it — a pear. But as you eat this pear, indeed as you begin to digest it, you forget that this pear actually came from someplace. This pear was once hanging from the branch of a pear tree, and then someone came along — it might have been a farmer, farmworker, farmhand — and plucked that pear from the branch of that pear tree.

And perhaps you recollect how it was you came to have this pear. It was at the end of a long day of work, and you were wheeling your shopping basket up and down the supermarket aisle; your mind was not even on shopping, was it? No. Your mind was elsewhere. Your mind was on why that fax did not come in at work; who's picking up the kids after school? Your mind was everywhere *but* on the pears, the tomatoes, the bananas, the box of eggs, the jug of milk that you are putting into your shopping basket.

And so you have forgotten entirely that you are ... *(Looks to audience for answer; someone says, "Shopping.")* Gathering food! Gathering food, something our ancestors, as far back as a million, 2 million, 3 million years have been gathering food.

And then when it comes time to eat the pear, we don't even say any word of thanks, do we? No, we have no sacrament. We've become so completely disconnected — we forget that this pear was once part of an ecosystem, was once hanging from the branch of a pear tree, and in all likelihood it was not an isolated pear tree, we can presume it was part of an orchard of pear trees and there were insects in the soil and microorganisms, and bees buzzing about to pollinate the trees; there was, you see, an entire web, an entire meta-structure, if you will, from which this pear sprang, before someone came along and — *(Long pause; addresses audience.)* No, don't get ahead of yourself! — *(Pause.)* plucked that pear from the branch of that pear tree.

And so we have been talking about — the pear. Or have we?! It's not just the pear, is it? No no, it's everything. This is the way we live, if you could call it living.

NARRATOR. After class, Rush Limbaugh again tried to catch up with Nina Eggly. But again he lost her in a sea of Ben & Jerry's T-shirts.

That night, Nina Eggly made a phone call to her friend Jenny Captanian.

NINA. *(On phone.)* Look, am I crazy? There's this guy in Spanish class who I'm kind of attracted to. No, he's not particularly good looking. I mean he does have a nice mustache and goatee beard. But he's the only one in the class who has any spark. *(Pause.)* No, he does not remind me of my father— well, maybe a little bit.

NARRATOR. **May 30, 1996**. Rush Limbaugh goes on the air.

RUSH. *(On air.)* This is the Rush Limbaugh Radio Program, and *(Takes bite.)* I'm eating a pear. Why am I eating a pear? I'll be right back to tell you.

(Working on Spanish during commercial break:) Solamente aspirina. Ayer me tomé cinco. Quítese la corbata y la camisa. Ponga —

(On air again.) We are back, and I am eating a pear. To demonstrate that we live in the Golden Age of Agriculture. America 1996: I challenge you in the history of the world to find a civilization with a system of agriculture that is as sophisticated as ours, as technological, as — agricultural.

The pear I am eating incidentally is not just any ordinary pear. This is a *genetically engineered* pear. 36 percent larger, 59 percent more pest-resistant, and it has a shelf life of 1.7 years. When we come back, Three Warning Signs of Liberalism.

NARRATOR. During the commercial break Rush Limbaugh marveled at how well his pear material went. As he was savoring the moment, an article in that morning's New York *Times* happened to catch his eye. That chance occurrence — the spotting of an intriguing newspaper article — was one Rush Limbaugh would live to regret.

RUSH. *(On air. Rattles newspaper.)* I am holding in my hand — this is choice! You're in for a treat. This is from today's New York *Times*, not a newspaper I generally quote from — in fact, if the New York *Times* were sacked and pillaged, I would not shed a tear. But here is an article that fits under the rubric on the Rush Limbaugh Program of "Leftover Lefties of the Sixties and What Has Become of Them."

Here on the front page, lemme just read. Mr. and Mrs. Delbert Brook of Cos Cob, Connecticut, are offering a reward of $1 million to anybody who can find their daughter ... *Jean* Brook. And Jean Brook is a Leftover Lefty of the Nineteen Sixties. A member of the Weather Underground, *the* most noxious anti-war — see, treason is too good a word — see, their idea was you rob banks, knock over Brinks security trucks, and somehow that was supposed to effectuate a U.S.

pullout from Vietnam. *That* is the level of thinking we're dealing with.

Jean Brook ... on the FBI's Most Wanted List ... her parents now in their eighties ... the father ailing; wants to see his daughter before he dies. Well now doesn't that just tug at your heartstrings?

That's not all. Article goes on to say, Mr. and Mrs. Brook offering a second reward, also $1 million, to Jean Brook *herself,* should she come forward, for her to turn over to the charity of her choice. The charity of her ch — Should we do something with this, Chris? Let's do a contest! Call it the "Leftover Lefty of the Sixties Charity Money Contest." And the question we want you to respond to: What would be the most appropriate charity for a Leftover Lefty of the Sixties? Send us your ideas!

And for the winners ... first-class airfare to New York, accommodations — can we do the Plaza, Chris? Yes! Luxury suite, New York's Plaza Hotel, and of course a three-day pass to be members of the Rush Limbaugh Entourage. As usual, winners chosen on the basis of originality and political incorrectness.

NARRATOR. That day, when Rush Limbaugh got off the air, he received a message to go directly to the office of his manager.

BARRY. Have a seat, Rush. You wanna cuppa coffee? Sit. I liked the pear bit, incidentally. The contest is brilliant. Now take a look at this fax. Are you at all familya with the New York Shakespeare Festival?

RUSH. They want me to do blackface?

BARRY. Rush, Othello — Othello is a black man.

RUSH. You want me to be the next Ted Danson?

BARRY. Rush, Rodriguez is up to 11.3.

RUSH. *(Holding script.)* "Most potent, grave and reverend Signiors, my very noble and approved ... " Is that the tone you're looking for, Spalding?

SPALDING GRAY. Rush, let's let's let's back up.

I was taking magic mushrooms one time, and I couldn't speak. I was in my manager's office, and I had no words left — for anything. And he said, "You should direct." And I said, "My *god*, you're right." And he said, "Go find the absolute — absolute other. Go find your shadow." And I, I, I thought, "Rush Limbaugh." And he was holding a very tall glass of iced lemonade — and I asked him to pour it over my head. He said, "Spalding, are you on drugs?" And I said, "As a matter of fact I *am*." And to his credit, he poured the lemonade over my head, and the ice cubes went down my my my collar.

RUSH. *(On air.)* See, that is where entrepreneurship really starts in America: kids selling lemonade. And now they want to regulate — I mean the Health Department — "Do you have a permit" — I mean, really, ladies and gentlemen, what did these lemonade-selling — I mean, did these kids put cyanide — Are these children Jim ... Jones?

When we come back, the most shining and victorious moment that you and I have shared as a radio program.

(Off air; pen in hand.) Dear Nina, Last night in class — No.

Querida Nina, Anoche en la clase tu di — dij — what's the past tense of *decir* ...

(On air again.) I am holding in my hand a telegram of congratulations from Senator Orrin Hatch — something you and I have been working on on this program steadfastly, assiduously for 4½ months; now I think with some degree of legitimacy we can claim victory. Because now it is the law of the land. I am speaking of course about the 1996 Federal Law Enforcement Supplemental Protection Act. So that beginning next week — see, now you don't have to kill, you don't have to shoot, you don't have to wound; if you so much as push — *push* — a Federal Law Enforcement Officer, you now face

a mandatory 10-year prison term. Finally, a little bit of respect for these dedicated men and women.

Yes, thank you, Chris. Got it right here. Ladies and gentlemen, we have our first winner in the Jean Brook Left-over Lefty Charity Money Contest. Our congratulations today go to Mr. Edwin Blucher, Corvallis, Oregon, who says the $1 million charity money should go the Paul Newman Spotted Owl College Scholarship Fund, which each year will send a deserving member of an endangered species to an elite Ivy League university, along with a year's supply of Newman's Own Spaghetti Sauce.

NARRATOR. **June 4, 1996.** The New School. Spanish teacher Gloria Escobar-Kittredge plans to show her Spanish class a film, *Nos Movemos: We Are Moving Ourselves,* which documents the alarming spread of aerobics classes in Puerto Rico. When she asks for a volunteer to get the projector, two students raise their hands: Nina Eggly and Russell Lindbergh. They agree to go together to the media lab.

Walking down the corridor, Rush Limbaugh entertains Nina Eggly with an impersonation of their Spanish teacher. Nina Eggly thinks of running her hand through Russell's hair, but then remembers that he doesn't have much hair. So instead, she kisses him on the lips.

8:30 P.M. After class, Rush Limbaugh and Nina Eggly wind their way through Greenwich Village, hands entwined; and Rush Limbaugh rediscovers the simple pleasure of walking down the street without an entourage. At his suggestion, they stop at a Häagen Dazs ice cream parlor.

RUSH. *(Holding ice cream cone and imitating Alvin Volt.)* And so, Nina, here you have an ice cream cone. But you, as an urban dweller, you forget that this ice cream cone actually came from someplace. And then someone came and *plucked* this ice cream cone from the Häagen Dazs tree.

NINA. And already we're eating our double chocolate macadamia nut ice cream cones. *(Imitating Alvin Volt.)* Without any word of thanks, because we have no sacrament.

RUSH. *(Imitating Daniel Horowitz.)* When I was in Cooba in '67, we went for over three months without ice cream.

NARRATOR. **9:19 P.M.** Rush Limbaugh and Nina Eggly have just made love in Nina's studio apartment in Greenwich Village. Now they share a post-coital pint of Ben & Jerry's ice cream. The flavor is Wavy Gravy.

NINA. Russell, why do you think some people like surprises and some don't?

RUSH. *Solamente en español, Señorita Eggly.*

NINA. Okay, *mi amiga Jenny y su novia — (Lapses back into English.)* my friend Jenny and her lover: they have these surprise dates. Like last week, Jenny got tickets to the k.d. lang concert at Carnegie Hall. And then on Thursday she went and picked up Martha after work and they got on the bus, and I mean Martha has no idea where they're going, it's a surprise; she doesn't even know if it's a movie or a play or a concert or maybe just dinner out. Anyway, they get off the bus, walk to Carnegie Hall, and Martha starts looking at the people waiting in line for the concert. And it looked like y'know a pretty dykey crowd, so she guessed it was a Ferron concert. Which I thought was pretty close.

RUSH. These two friends of yours, Jenny and Martha — uh — uh ...

NARRATOR. Rush Limbaugh wants to ask Nina Eggly if her friends are lesbians, but is unable to.

RUSH. *(Swallowing.)* Jenny and Martha, how do you know them?

NINA. I know Jenny from Santa Fe, we were in a women's journal-writing support group.

RUSH. Oh! Only women in the group!

NINA. Actually, there were a couple of guys — we kicked them out. *(Laughs.)* I mean, I was okay with having them; Jenny always says I'm too accepting of men. Of course, there *was* a time when I was ready to kill all men. I think that was during the Ford Administration.

NARRATOR. As he listens to her speak, Rush Limbaugh looks around the room. He sees a Guerrilla Girls poster, a signed first edition of *Our Bodies, Ourselves,* and a framed photograph of Bella Abzug. Slowly it dawns on him that he has just gone to bed with a feminist. Rush Limbaugh feels dizzy and reaches for the table to steady himself. A voice inside his head tells him to leave the apartment at once, but then he sees the dimples in her cheeks. He stays, telling himself that he needs Nina to help him learn Spanish.

NINA. And then I met Walt. Walt Walt Walt. You know, the day Walt told me he was sleeping with Cherisse, was I think the angriest I've ever been in my entire life. Eighteen years together! Two kids! And what does he say? "It's biological. Men need to be allowed to fuck more than one woman." And then he backs it up with something from Joseph Campbell. And, you know, the thing that was so humiliating for me, was I thought I had put all the anger behind me. I mean, I had stopped talking about patriarchy and the legitimate rage of all women. Everything was about healing and letting go — letting go! *(Picks up phone.)* Hello? Oh hi! Yeah, oh right! No no, that's okay. We'll do it another time. That's actually better. Okay. Okay. Okay. Bye. *(Hangs up. Pause.)* Huh. What a coincidence. Remember in Millennial Musings, that Rush Limbaugh person who I'd never heard of?

RUSH. Yeah, the uh talk show personality.

NINA. Right. Well, my friend Jenny does costumes for the New York Shakespeare Festival, where this Rush Limbaugh person is evidently playing Othello. Anyway, there's this big rehearsal going on now and Rush Limbaugh is not there and he didn't call, and so Jenny — Russell, are you going someplace?

NARRATOR. In hindsight, it appears that this lateness incident was the moment things began to unravel for Rush Limbaugh. Barry Granatour recalls what happened ...

BARRY. *(Retrospect interview.)* They had phoned me at the office: "Where's Rush?" — and everything I tried, there was no answer. The phone, the beeper, the limo — *nada.* So I personally go down to the rehearsal at the Delacorte Theater in Central Park; first thing I see when I get there is the guy playing Iago — Garrison Keillor.

GARRISON KEILLOR. *(As Iago.)* I have looked upon the world for four times seven years and since I could distinguish between a benefit and an injury I never found man that knew how to love himself.... Drown thyself! Drown cats and blind puppies! *(Long inhalation.)*

BARRY. *(Retrospect interview.)* Now! There was a very large crowd gathered around Jackie Mason. Jackie Mason who was in the production, cast as — now I'm trying to remember. Roderigo! Roderigo! Anyway, so Mason's got a crowd of people around him, and what's he doing? — he's working up some new material.

JACKIE MASON. You go to any bookstore, you look at all the books on all the shelves: why is it that 99 percent of all the books are written by Jews? Because in a Jewish family, everybody's always talking at the same time. *"Don't eat that!"* "I'm going to eat it!" *"You can't eat it, it has cholesterol!"* "But it's good cholesterol!" *"Bad cholesterol!"* "Good cholesterol!" *"Bad —"*

And a certain percentage of Jews get tired of being interrupted and they want to finish what they're saying; and so they write a book!

Which is the complete opposite of White Anglo Saxon Gentiles. In a White Anglo Saxon Gentile family, nobody talks. All year long they say maybe three woids. Then one time a year, at Christmas, they have a conversation. "When should we open the presents?"

Most Gentile children do not talk before the age of 18. This is a fact.

Which explains the phenomenon of our fellow actor Mr. Rush Limbaugh. Why is Rush Limbaugh the only talk show host in the woild who never has a guest? Because for him talking is still a novelty, and he can't get over it.

Which is exactly the same situation as Garrison Keillor: you ever listen to Garrison Keillor's program on the radio? What that man does on the radio: he could never get away with in a Jewish family. Opens up his mouth, he says maybe six woids, and then he comes up for air. "Vell, it's been a quiet week ..." *(Inhales very deeply.)*

In a Jewish family inhaling like that is a big mistake: you'll never finish your sentence. "No, it was not a quiet week, what are you talking about, it was a noisy week!"

NARRATOR. Later that night Nina Eggly received another phone call from her friend Jenny Captanian.

NINA. Wait a minute: this is *after* showing up two hours late for rehearsal?! He won't let you take his measurements because he wants it done by someone who's *not* a man-hater? *(Laughs.)* Well, Jen, it sounds like this Limbaugh guy sure has your number, huh? *(Pause.)* No, no, I'm sorry I said that. It *was* insensitive.

Jen, look, you cannot let this Limbaugh person get to you this way. You've got to do something with the anger, you know, find some way to transform the energy.

NARRATOR. **June 5, 1996.** Millennial Musings. The lecture that night is given by the Israeli somatic feminist, Elea Avón.

ELEA AVÓN. Before anything else I would like you to please get very comfortable. Feel your bottom on your chair.

When you look around the island of Manhattan, what do you see? You see heads bobbing around; am I correct, people? This is what you see, yes? Really! I'm talking about *you!* Sitting there as if you are only a head and do not have any — body!

Feel your bodies, people. Feel them!

Feel your arms, feel your hands — *(Points to an audience member.)* Good! Feel the fingers as they come out of your hands. *(Points to an audience member.)* Very good! Do you know what your hands are for — evolutionarily speaking? They are not for punching numbers in computer. They're for making stone tools! Feel your bodies. Feel your legs. Evolutionarily — for running! Women, feel your breasts! Stick them out! Do you realize what this society has done to breasts? This society has taken breasts ... and has pasted them on billboards to sell Calvin Klein linguhree. I have some news for you people: that is not what breasts are for! Form follows function. Really! There's a nipple at the end; that's where the milk comes out. A breast is to suckle a baby.

Feel your genitalia!

We live in a stupid century. The 20th century is the stupidest century there has ever been. Really! Super machines! What have we created in 20th century? Supercollider, supercomputer, superconductor. Super super super super super. But we have forgotten, completely forgotten in 20th century, about our super *bodies!* Feel your genitalia — *now!* Is there anyone here tonight who can tell me what are the two purposes, evolutionarily speaking, for your genitalia? *(She scans the audience for an answer.)*

NARRATOR. *(Before any answers have been offered by audience members.)* After class, at her apartment, Nina Eggly gives Rush Limbaugh a massage.

RUSH. Oh yes! Mmm. Wait, hold on a sec, Nina. You hear that up there, your neighbor's radio? Nina, mind if I turn on your radio? *(He turns on the radio.)*

J. NEIL RODRIGUEZ. ... treating cancer patients — and these are federally funded programs, *mis amigos,* my friends! And that is today's big question, *The Big ¿Porque? of the Day* on the J. Neil H-r-r-r-odriguez Program, is why — why why why why why — why should you and I pay with our federal tax dollars — for so-called alternative cancer therapies: acupuncture, visualization, breathing exercises, massage! Tell me, who in their right mind would treat cancer with *massage?!*

NINA. Russell, turn it off.

RUSH. No, Nina, I want to hear this.

RODRIGUEZ. Now let's go to our phone. The number that you call ...

NINA. Russell, what are you doing?

RODRIGUEZ. Talk to me, America! Agree, disagree, make me laugh, make me cry, *pero no me aburras:* don't bore me, America!!

RUSH. *(Holding telephone in one hand, and pinching his nose with the thumb and forefinger of the other hand.)* Yes, this is Roland in Manhattan, and I have a cancer experience I think is relevant. Yes, I will hold for Mr. Rodriguez. *(Covering mouthpiece of telephone with hand.)* Nina, watch what I do to this guy.

RODRIGUEZ. Roland in Manhattan, *you* are on the J. Neil H-r-r-rodriguez Program.

RUSH/ROLAND. *(Holding phone and nose.)* First, I'd like to say I listen to your program whenever I can: at home, in the car, in the operating room.

RODRIGUEZ. Hold on, hold on, hold on, sir, you are, I take it, in the *medical* profession?

RUSH/ROLAND. *(Holding phone and nose.)* Yes, that's correct, I am — an oncologist.

RODRIGUEZ. An oncologist! An oncologist! Ring the bell, Marylou! *(He rings the bell himself.)* This is the first time to my knowledge that an oncologist has called in to the J. Neil H-r-r-rodriguez Program. And do you have a comment, doctor, about these so-called alternative cancer therapies?

RUSH/ROLAND. *(Holding phone and nose.)* I would not be speaking to you today, sir, if it were not for massage. Four years ago I had pancreatic cancer ...

RODRIGUEZ. Hold on, hold on, hold on. You are a cancer doctor who yourself had cancer! Ring the bell, Marylou! *(He rings the bell.)* A cancer doctor who himself had cancer!

RUSH/ROLAND. *(Holding phone and nose.)* Upon diagnosis my own oncologist told me I had just six months to live. Then, against his advice, I began receiving intensive *massage* treatments, four to six hours every day. Can I prove they cured me? No. Can you prove that they did *not* cure me? No. I'm still alive today. I think they did.

RODRIGUEZ. Sir, were you additionally taking chemotherapy or radiation?

RUSH/ROLAND. *(Holding phone and nose.)* You know what your problem is, J. Neil Rodriguez? You live in a stupid century. See, in this century we've forgotten all about our super *bodies* and their ability to heal themselves. Oh excuse me, I'm being paged. I have a bone marrow transplant on the 9th floor! Gotta go. *(Hangs up.)*

NINA. *(Laughing.)* Do you call these shows a lot?

RUSH. Call them? No. Not a *whole* lot. You know, the one I really do want to call is that Rush Limbaugh. He's the one with the largest audience. You really oughta listen to him sometime, Nina. You know, for class, for Millennial Musings. So! You ready to get started on irregular verbs? *(Blackout. In the dark.)* Nina! Oh! Mmmmm. *(Sound of phones ringing: a public TV pledge break.)*

ARNOLD PLEDGE. You know, you just don't get programming like this anywhere else. And that's why we're asking you now to go to your phones, help support public television, KQED Channel 9. Where you get programs *like* this *Frontline* documentary, like *Masterpiece Theater* and *Nova*; next month we've got the new five-part John Bradshaw series on healing from the loss of an area code. We *are* going to take a brief intermission now, and then, just as soon as we've raised our goal of $17,835, we'll go ahead and present the conclusion of this *Frontline* documentary. *(Fade to black.)*

End of Act One

ACT TWO

BARRY. *(Retrospect interview.)* Now, at the time I had no idea there was a woman that Rush had become involved with. Nor did I know that this Roland who became a regular caller on the Rodriguez program was actually Rush with his fingers over his nose.

You have to remember that all this was going on in the *context* of the 1996 Presidential campaign. And every day Rush was going on the air and viciously attacking Clinton. And in fact Clinton was trailing very, very badly in the polls. Of course that was before the asteroid scare.

BBC NEWSCASTER. Beep beep beep beep beeeeep. It's oh-three hours Greenwich Mean Time. BBC World Service. The News, read by Thomas Obreviture. First the main points:

An asteroid the size of Pakistan has narrowly missed hitting the Earth. Scientists say the asteroid Bob-17, which came within 29 miles of the Earth's gravitational orbit, would have caused property damage estimated in the thousands of millions of pounds, as well as the destruction of the human species.

NARRATOR. **June 12, 1996.** In an Oval Office speech, President Clinton unveils a $44.9 trillion anti-asteroid shield. In the 11-minute address, Clinton invokes the name of God 39 times. Within a day Clinton climbs in the polls from 31 to 67 percent. Political analyst Booth Percy.

BOOTH PERCY. The two big winners in the asteroid scare were Bill Clinton and J. Neil Rodriguez. Clinton had finally found something big enough to distract people from the scandal around Chelsea's orthodontia.

Rodriguez completely lampooned Clinton's asteroid shield. He said, "Why should we pay 45 trillion dollars to essentially reduce our stress when we could use the same money to buy everyone on earth a hot tub and a large-screen TV?"

That was his *Big Porque of the Week.*

RUSH. *(On air.)* This is the Rush Limbaugh Program and when we come back, more on the gay performance artist Homo Ludens.

(Off air, working on Othello lines, trying to get them straight.) Oh now forever

Farewell the tranquil mind! Farewell content!
Farewell the neighing steed …
Farewell the ear-piercing fife …

(On air again.) I'm going to get to Homo Ludens in a moment, but first there's been an awful lotta stuff in the news lately about this new automatic condom, the so-called "airbag." Which has been available on the shelves of pharmacies for some eight weeks. *Eight weeks,* and already some people talking about putting these things into — high schools!

See, there are two simple English words — oh, you know I'd get in so much trouble if I said 'em. Can't say 'em! See, it has become taboo, politically inco — *(Looks at control booth.)* What's that? Chris wants me to say them one time. No! Not gonna do it. *(Raps knuckles on table.)* Homo Ludens — *(Looks at control booth.)* Whisper them?! Chris wants me to whisper them one time. You got me on the ropes, Chris. I'm wavering. Ladies and gentlemen, my engineer Mr. Chris French has beaten me into submission and I now have no choice but to whisper — I'm only gonna do it one time! One time, one time only! Thereafter you will never again hear Rush Limbaugh say these two words over the air, so please listen closely. *(Big pause; leans in, whispers:)* Teenage abstinence.

(Loud.) "You can't say that, Limbaugh!" Every liberal, every permissivist: "You cannot say —" I'm not gonna say 'em! Not, not, not, never, never, just said 'em for the first and last — in fact, in fact, in fact, from now on, ladies and gentlemen, from now on I will simply say — *(Pause; he leans in; quietly:)* "Teen-ab." *(Pause.)* You and I will know what I am talking about.

Yes, thank you, Chris. Got it right here. We have, ladies and gentlemen, we have our next winner in the Jean Brook Leftover Lefty of the Sixties Charity Money Contest. You got any fanfare cued up, Chris? No fanfare! Well, I'll do it myself. Bum puh-puh bum-bum pum pum. Our congratulations today go to Mrs. Lenore DeMarco, Fort Collins, Colorado. Mrs. DeMarco writes that the $1 million charity money should be donated to the Berkeley Relocation Society, a non-profit organization dedicated to airlifting the entire city of Berkeley, California, including its fine university — to Havana, Cooba! And obviously, Mrs. DeMarco, you wrote your entry before last Tuesday, and it's true, we now have 73,000 of our finest, bravest U.S. Marines in Cooba helping to engineer at last a transition to Cooban democracy, but Mrs. DeMarco, notwithstanding that, I like the way your mind works!

NARRATOR. **The evening of June 13, 1996.** Rush Limbaugh attends dress rehearsal for *Othello* at the Delacorte Theater in Central Park. There, work begins on the play's final scene, the scene in which Othello *suffocates* Desdemona.

RUSH. *(As Othello.)* When I have plucked the rose,
I cannot give it vital growth again,
It needs must wither. I'll smell it on the tree. *(Kisses Desdemona.)*

SPALDING GRAY. Rush, let's start over. I was in Thailand, and I was introduced to a very wealthy man. Who was very much concerned about his appearance. He would change his clothes every two hours. He wore these beautiful silk robes, they were purple and they had embroidered buttons. And every two hours he would say, "Take these away. I want new ones."

And finally I said to him, "Don't you think you should grow up?" I mean, I am as compulsive as the next guy; but I am aware of my compulsions.

RUSH. Spalding, why are you telling me this?

SPALDING GRAY. Rush, you know what your problem is —

I had a dentist's appointment and the technician who came in to do the cleaning — a black man, much like Othello. He looked in my mouth and he said: "There's plaque. Do you know you have — plaque?" Now there were many things I was aware of about myself, but I had no idea that one of them was — plaque.

NARRATOR. **9:21 P.M.** Rush Limbaugh stops behind a bush in Central Park to affix his false mustache and goatee beard. He has just stormed out of rehearsal after an argument with Spalding Gray. Now he hails a taxicab and heads downtown to Nina Eggly's apartment in Greenwich Village. While he is in the taxicab, Nina Eggly receives a phone call from Jenny Captanian.

NINA. Next Wednesday, opening night, *(Delighted, laughing.)* twenty women all dressed as — Jenny, this is brilliant! Right, and since it's opening night, the critics — oh, you are going to get so much publicity. This is wonderful! Wait a minute, I think someone's at the door. *(Looks toward door.)* Oh, Russell! *(On phone.)* Jen, it's Russell, I should go. Love you too. Bye. *(Hangs up. Playfully.)* Russell, before I forget, next Wednesday, at — 4:30 in the afternoon, I need you to be here. And I'm not going to tell you what for. *(She kisses him.)*

RUSH. Nina, I cannot wait till Wednesday. Let's get out of here *tonight.* Before the next asteroid comes and wipes us all out. How about the Bahamas?

NINA. I'd love to. Or Mexico — work on our Spanish. *(Phone rings.)* Oh, let the machine get it. — Or Peru, I've always wanted to see Macchu Pi— Wait, this is my daughter, I need to get this. *(Picks up phone.)* I'm here, Sunset! You okay? *(Pause.)* Oh, honey. Sweetie, I love you very much. Do you want me to come be with you? I can take the next plane — *(Pause.)* No, I'm your mother. This is important. Honey, how far along —? Just six weeks. Have you told your father? Yes, I'll wait. *(Pause. To Russell.)* My daughter is pregnant. She has call waiting.

NARRATOR. That night, Nina Eggly takes a midnight plane to Chicago to be with her daughter. She is accompanied on United flight 327 by her lover, Russell Lindbergh. As they board the plane, Russell notices a familiar-looking man sitting in the first-class section.

RUSH. That guy with the dark glasses and pencil mustache: I've seen him somepl — Wait. The New School! He sat next to me in Millennial Musings!

NINA. What a coincidence.

NARRATOR. Takeoff is delayed for over two hours because of unexpected local thunderstorms.

NINA. Oh, I forgot to tell you. I finally listened to Rush Limbaugh today.

RUSH. Oh!! What'd you think?

NINA. Has anybody ever told you, he sounds a little bit like you? Anyway, it's true, his politics are really lousy. But — he did this thing about Homo Ludens, y'know, the gay performance artist with the whole NEA grant controversy: the guy who goes on stage with a picture of Jesse Helms and pees on it? Anyway, so what Rush Limbaugh does is he says, "I am *so* offended by Homo Ludens. I am *so* offended by Homo Ludens." He says it over and over, I don't know, eight times, this big crescendo, "I am *so* offended ..." Then finally he says, "I am so offended because Homo Ludens has never peed on *my* picture. I keep sending him glossy photographs of myself for him to pee on ..."

I'm not doing it very well. The guy's a satirist. He's a little bit like Homo Ludens. Homo Ludens pees on Jesse Helms. Rush Limbaugh pees on Homo Ludens. I don't know, it's what boys do to each other. *(Rush looks startled.)*

NARRATOR. The plane finally leaves the ground at 2:26 A.M. New York time.

NINA. Sunset's a great kid but she got involved with one of her professors, a guy in the art department. And they used one of those "automatic condoms" — never inflated. Not that

I didn't do some pretty dumb stuff when I was her age.

NARRATOR. Nina begins telling him the story of her life: her childhood as Jean Brook, her years in the Weather Underground, her subsequent life under an assumed name.

Rush Limbaugh reaches overhead to open his air vent. But the flow of air does nothing to quiet the throbbing at the back of his skull. Should he turn her in to the authorities? Should he tell her that her parents are looking for her? Should he reveal to her *his own* true identity?

But the question that comes out of his mouth is a different one entirely:

RUSH. Are you — going to eat those peanuts?

NINA. Russell, you know, you're the only person I've ever told about this. Don't — turn me in, OK?

RUSH. Isn't it hard — living a double life?

NINA. For the first ten years it drove me completely nuts. Especially when Sunset was little — I thought, I'm denying her her grandparents. Of course then I remembered my father would never have anything to do with grandchildren who weren't white.

And god!, you know, underneath everything there was always this layer of paranoia that at any time somebody might figure out who I was and turn me in. There was a time the paranoia got so intense — I remember it was right around Sunset's third birthday, I was still pregnant with Shiatsu. And I mean I was immobilized by the fear.

Finally I went and saw this shaman, this Taos Indian man named Crying Eagle. He took me up to the top of Taos Mountain and I had brought with me this old photograph of myself as a little girl, with my mom and dad and sister, all of us standing in front of the Christmas tree. And at sunset Crying Eagle lit some cedar and some sage. And I took the photograph and I held it over the burning cedar; and I let go. And I watched the smoke. And then Crying Eagle said — he said: "We die many times, we have many griefs. We continue." *(Short pause.)* He gave me a quartz crystal. The same one I still wear.

And after that, I was okay with it. I *was* Nina Eggly.

NARRATOR. For a moment Russell Lindbergh considers what would happen if he tried the same thing — a ceremony to let go of his old identity as Rush Limbaugh. He imagines himself holding a blue-and-orange armband over a fire of burning cedar. He imagines a new life, in a new country — perhaps Denmark — an ordinary life, in which he and Nina Eggly are letter carriers in a small town, delivering the mail by bicycle, getting into really good shape, staying up late together working on their Danish pronouns. Rush Limbaugh is drawn farther and farther into this dream of a new life. But then the captain turns on the "Fasten Seat Belts" sign, and announces the local weather and time.

O'Hare Airport. While Nina Eggly uses the restroom, Rush Limbaugh calls his manager's voice mail.

RUSH. Barry, Rush. Look. Working very hard on my *español;* I will not be in this morning. Put on a rerun. Oh — and call Spalding. Tell him if he ever wants to see me again — no more stories!

NARRATOR. **Evanston, Illinois.** Rush Limbaugh and Nina Eggly prepare to sleep on the floor of Sunset Eggly's college dorm room. Lying under the down comforter, Rush Limbaugh again sees the image of the burning blue-and-orange armband. Then he looks at the woman sleeping next to him, and a tear rolls down his cheek. Rush Limbaugh leans over and lightly kisses the sleeping Nina Eggly.

Monday, June 17, 1996. New York City. Rush Limbaugh is now in a taxicab heading from LaGuardia Airport to his broadcast studios in midtown Manhattan. He looks at his watch and sees that he's late.

RUSH. *(Urgent.)* What's going on; why is there so much traffic today?

CAB DRIVER. *Lo siento, no hablo ingles.*

RUSH. Okay, *español. (Falteringly.) ¿Porque no podemos — movernos — en este — trafficojam?*

CAB DRIVER. *Aaah, los Limbaughistas! ¿No ha oido? Hay un gran tumulto.*

NARRATOR. As Rush Limbaugh tries to figure out the meaning of the word "Limbaughistas," he sees a group of looters run by, carrying computer terminals, telephones, Scotch tape dispensers. They are wearing the blue-and-orange armbands of the Rush Limbaugh Entourage. Limbaugh leaves the cab and runs up to his broadcast studio.

BARRY. Rush, where the hell have you been? You didn't show on time, they went crazy. The whole Entourage! What they did to the offices of The New York *Times!* What they did wi — *(Points to ON AIR sign and mouths the following words:)* Rush, you're on the air!

RUSH. This is the Rush Limbaugh Program, and let's go right to our telephone lines. Cos Cob, Connecticut, *you* are on the Rush Limbaugh Program.

DELBERT BROOK. *(Fragile.)* Mr. Limbaugh, my name is Delbert Brook. I am the father of Jean Brook, whom you refer to as a "leftover lefty of the sixties." I refer to her as my daughter. Sir, what you are doing to my family is cruel, and I ask you now to stop it.

RUSH. *(In shock; pause; with effort:)* Commercial. *(He walks, staggering, a few steps.)*

BARRY. Rush, did I mention that Rodriguez is up to 19? Ever since this Roland guy has been calling in, his ratings have gone through the fucking roof!

NARRATOR. **Wednesday, June 19, 1996. 12:51 P.M.** Spalding Gray writes in his diary: "Tonight we open the definitive *Othello.*"

2:37 P.M. Barry Granatour sells ABC Television exclusive rights to a backstage, Barbara Walters interview of Rush Limbaugh as Othello.

3:09 P.M. Delbert and Harriet Brook, acting on a tip,

begin driving from Cos Cob, Connecticut to New York City.

3:22 P.M. J. Neil Rodriguez begins secret talks with programming executives at ABC Television.

3:27 P.M. Jenny Captanian distributes costumes and goes over plans with 21 fellow members of the women's direct action collective Pants on Fire.

4:03 P.M. Opening night of *Othello* now less than four hours away. As he showers, Rush Limbaugh agonizes over whether to keep his 4:30 P.M. date with Nina Eggly. Soon his mind drifts back to one of the Millennial Musings lectures: the lecture given by the Indian philosopher Dr. Ginta Rosh.

GINTA ROSH. Transformation. People think transformation is very complicated. Not complicated. Simple. You want to understand transformation, watch a snake. Watch a snake shed its skin. That is all you need to know about transformation.

NARRATOR. In the shower, Limbaugh's mind returns to the dream of a new life as a Danish letter carrier. Then Limbaugh bolts naked out of the shower.

RUSH. *(Picks up phone.)* Yeah, SAS, when's your next flight to Copenhagen? 6:25 tonight: perfect! I need two tickets, first-class, the name is Lindbergh, as in the aviator. Traveling companion: Eggly, E-G-G-L-Y.

NARRATOR. Limbaugh towels dry, dresses, takes a cab to Nina Eggly's apartment.

RUSH. Nina, pack your bag, we're going to Europe tonight! I've got the tickets!

NINA. Russell, I can't get a passport. I'm a fugitive. But I do have a little surprise for *you.*

NARRATOR. Nina Eggly blindfolds Russell Lindbergh and leads him to the I.N.D. subway on a surprise date.

5:15 P.M. Nina and Russell arrive at their destination, and Nina removes the blindfold.

RUSH. Central Park!

NINA. Sit down, Russell! I've got a picnic in my backpack, and Jenny has gotten us tickets to the opening night of *Othello!*

It's right over there, in the Delacorte Theater.

NARRATOR. Rush Limbaugh feels dizzy. He excuses himself and walks to the men's room. But the men's room is locked. Limbaugh passes a picnicking couple fervently kissing and caressing, pausing only to take bites of a Bosc pear. Limbaugh walks on, aimlessly, trying to figure out what to do. He is approached by an elderly couple.

DELBERT BROOK. Excuse me, sir, we're looking for the Delacorte Theater.

NARRATOR. Limbaugh points them to the theater and keeps walking. He has no way of knowing the people he just encountered: Delbert and Harriet Brook.

NINA. *(Catching sight of Russell and waving to him.)* Oh, Russell, there you are.

RUSH. Nina, there's something I need to tell you. I need to tell you that —

NARRATOR. Now he intends to tell her the truth: that he is not Russell Lindbergh, but Rush Limbaugh; that he must play Othello that night in the Delacorte Theater. He *intends* to tell her this. But at the last moment, he falters.

RUSH. Nina, I need to tell you that — my mother's in a coma.

NINA. Oh, Russell.

RUSH. Yeah. I gotta go.

NINA. I'll come with you.

RUSH. We're not married. She won't like that.

NINA. How will she know? She's in a coma.

RUSH. Nina, no.

NARRATOR. Rush Limbaugh starts to leave, but Nina Eggly calls him back.

NINA. Russell, take this. It will protect you.

NARRATOR. Nina Eggly hangs her quartz crystal necklace around Russell's neck, and kisses him goodbye.

6:41 P.M. Rush Limbaugh stops behind a bush to remove his false mustache and goatee beard. He considers removing the quartz crystal necklace as well, but in the end decides to leave it on. Limbaugh arrives backstage at 6:54 P.M. There Jenny Captanian begins his makeup, working to darken the skin on Limbaugh's face and forearms.

7:57 P.M. Rush Limbaugh peeks out from behind the wings and he sees that the house is full. Then he spots, sitting in the second row, the elderly couple to whom he gave directions, and just behind them, a familiar-looking man with dark glasses and a pencil mustache. In rows 4 through 6 Limbaugh sees blue-and-orange armbands. And off to the side, he recognizes the Millennial Musings lecturers Elea Avón and Alvin Volt.

8:09 P.M. The curtain rises on *Othello.*

JACKIE MASON. *(As Roderigo.)* Tush, never tell me, I take it much unkindly

That thou, Iago, who hast had my purse as if the strings were thine

Shouldst know of this.

NARRATOR. **8:21 P.M.** Act One, Scene 2. Accompanied by Garrison Keillor and two torchbearers, Limbaugh walks onstage for the first time. Immediately the Rush Limbaugh Entourage begins stamping their feet and chanting in unison: "Limbaugh! Lim-baugh! Lim-baugh!" Three minutes and 18 seconds later, the eruption dies down and the play resumes.

8:32 P.M. Rush Limbaugh has just survived his first appearance of the night without missing a single line. He exits stage right.

RUSH. *(Hums happily to himself; then:)* And so here you have Othello. *(Imitating Alvin Volt.)* But you, as an urban dweller — you forget this Othello actually came from someplace. And then someone came along and plucked Othello from the Shakespeare tree.

NINA. Russell??

NARRATOR. In the dim backstage light, Limbaugh makes out the figure of a familiar woman.

RUSH. *(Pause.)* I'm sorry, I don't know you. Are you involved in this production?

NINA. I'm sorry, I thought you were someone else. Yeah, I'm with Jenny Captanian in costumes.

NARRATOR. Rush Limbaugh walks to make his next entrance. He cannot shake the question of what Nina Eggly is doing backstage.

RUSH. *(As Othello.)* Most potent, grave and reverend signiors, my very noble and approved good masters. *(Pause. Lost, he repeats, to himself:)* And — approved — good masters.

NARRATOR. For a moment there is silence. Then the silence is filled by the Rush Limbaugh Entourage, who again take up their chant: "Lim-baugh! Lim-baugh! Lim-baugh!" Limbaugh looks offstage to the prompter. He cannot hear him. All he hears is the Entourage. At the end of the scene Limbaugh exits shaking. He is bathed in sweat, and must have his blackface retouched.

Limbaugh returns to his dressing room and is blinded by television lights. It's the ABC crew; they begin shooting at once. Limbaugh scans the room; he's looking for Barbara Walters. But the person holding the microphone is a man Limbaugh has never seen before.

RODRIGUEZ. Good evening, *muy buenas noches, mis amigos,* my friends, coming to you live from backstage at New York's Delacorté Theater, I am J. Neil H-r-r-rodriguez and my guest …

NARRATOR. Limbaugh turns and walks out of his dressing room.

RUSH. Barry!

BARRY. *(Retrospect interview.)* To this day, I have never received a satisfactory explanation of why the hell Barbara Walters was not there.

NARRATOR. **10:17 P.M.** Act Five, Scene 2. Desdemona, played by Cokie Roberts, lies in bed.

COKIE ROBERTS. *(As Desdemona.)* I never gave him token.

RUSH. *(As Othello.)* By heaven, I saw *my* handkerchief in *his* hand!

NARRATOR. **10:18 P.M.**

RUSH *(As Othello.)* Down, strumpet!

COKIE ROBERTS. *(As Desdemona.)* Kill me tomorrow, let me live tonight!

RUSH. *(As Othello.)* It is too late.

NARRATOR. Cokie Roberts leans back on the bed and prepares to be suffocated by Rush Limbaugh. Rush Limbaugh reaches for Cokie Roberts' neck, but at that moment, he feels himself thrown backwards. Limbaugh hits his head on the hard wooden bedframe. Then, looking up from the bed, he sees not one but 23 Desdemonas, all wearing identical nightgowns. The Desdemonas form a circle and lift the bed high in the air, Cokie Roberts and Rush Limbaugh still on board. Then the Desdemonas begin chanting: "No more silence: We interrupt men's violence! Limbaugh, Othello: We'll turn your dick to jello!"

Hearing this, the Rush Limbaugh Entourage leaps onto the stage, 80 blue-and-orange armbands flashing wildly in the lights; they're heading straight for the Desdemonas.

Barry Granatour runs in from the wings, puts himself *between* the Desdemonas and the Entourage.

BARRY. T-shirts! Free T-shirts!

NARRATOR. The glare of the lights becomes suddenly brighter. It's the ABC crew.

RODRIGUEZ. *(Jams microphone in Limbaugh's face.)* A comment, Mr. Limbaugh, on what is occurring here in Act Five, Scene 2 of *Othello*?

NARRATOR. Before Limbaugh can answer, one of the Desdemonas sees the TV camera, jumps up on the bed and strips off her nightgown.

RODRIGUEZ. A man! A man! This Desdemona is a man! A naked man! Ring the bell, Marylou! *(He rings the bell.)*

HOMO LUDENS. So, Rush, you've been wanting me to pee on you?

NARRATOR. Rush Limbaugh looks up from the bed and sees the naked Homo Ludens preparing to urinate on him. Limbaugh scrambles to the edge of the bed, trying to escape. Homo Ludens grabs Limbaugh by the shirt, but the flimsy material gives way, and a small quartz crystal glitters in the bright lights as Limbaugh falls from the bed into the arms of three of the Desdemonas — including Nina Eggly.

NINA. *(Pause.)* Russell??!!

RUSH. Nina, I can explain everything.

NARRATOR. A tall man with a pencil mustache and dark glasses steps onstage, flashing an FBI badge.

FBI AGENT. Jean Brook, you are under arrest.

NARRATOR. An old man in the second row rises from his chair …

DELBERT BROOK. My God, Jean, is that you?!

NARRATOR. … and collapses. The FBI agent begins dragging Jean Brook away. Rush Limbaugh pushes the FBI agent off the stage.

RUSH. *(Pushes FBI Agent.)* You leave this woman alone! This is a good woman!

SPALDING GRAY. Rush, I like this *a lot.* Forget everything I said in rehearsal and go with what you're doing.

JACKIE MASON. Why is it that you can't go the theater in New York anymore and get the play that you paid for? You pay for *Othello,* you should get *Othello!* You should not get two dozen Desdemonas and a Rush Limbaugh Entourage!

ELEA AVÓN. *(In audience.)* What I like about this *Othello* is, it's so physical! Look at them: they're all in their bodies! That one is naked!

ALVIN VOLT. *(In audience.)* And so for the past two hours you've been watching *Othello.* But your mind has not *been* on *Othello,* has it? No, your mind's been elsewhere. Why was that dinner salad so small? But now suddenly the audience have become the actors and you're thrust back into the moment.

NINA. Russell, my father!

RUSH. Is there a doctor in the house?

HOMO LUDENS. *I'm* a doctor!

BARRY. *(Retrospect interview.)* It so happened that Homo Ludens, in addition to being a performance artist, is a physician.

NARRATOR. Rush Limbaugh instructs his entourage to pass Homo Ludens from hand to hand, down from the stage to the second row. There, still naked, Homo Ludens administers CPR to Delbert Brook and saves his life.

FBI AGENT. Rush Limbaugh, you are under arrest.

RUSH. Me? What did *I* do? *(Blackout. Lights come up on BBC Newscaster.)*

BBC NEWSCASTER. Beep beep beep beep beeeep. It's oh-three hours Greenwich Mean Time. An American production of *Othello* has ended in disarray, with a prominent talk show host and an elusive activist being held in custody.

BARRY. *(Retrospect interview.)* Rush's chief defense lawyer was Johnnie Cochran, which incidentally was my idea. But the fact that Rush had violated the 1996 Federal Law Enforcement Supplemental Protection Act which he had virtually *written* — the media crucified him. Jean Brook got off. When it came to light about her WANTED poster with Edgar Hoover in the dress, they quietly dropped the charges. She did get a million dollars from her father, which she used to establish a foundation: the Foundation for the Ethical Use of Satire. Do I think it was a mistake to put Rush in *Othello?* Absolutely not. Nor to send him to the New School for Spanish. No. See, you must always keep a celebrity on his toes. Which I do today with Neil Rodriguez.

DELBERT BROOK. *(Retrospect interview.)* I was delighted to have an opportunity to see my daughter again, and particularly to be present at the birth of my first great-grandchild, Biko.

SPALDING GRAY. *(Retrospect interview.)* I am working on *two* monologues based on what happened. The first one is called

The Definitive Othello, and the second one is going to be called *23 Desdemonas Led the Big Parade.*

GARRISON KEILLOR. *(Retrospect interview.)* And so that phrase, that you find at the very end of *Othello*, where Othello says, "Then you must speak of one that loved not wisely, but too well." Nina Eggly and Rush Limbaugh: two people who loved each other not wisely but too well. But you look at them today: one of them has her own foundation; the other one is eligible for parole in *three* years. And you realize that life — is pretty good.

NINA. *(Retrospect interview.)* When I found out who he really was, I was furious. And then I realized how desperate he must have been to get out of the box he'd put himself in as Rush Limbaugh. And how desperate I was to find someone who could make me laugh.

ALVIN VOLT. *(Retrospect interview.)* All of our Western systems of belief tell us that if you travel the 39 blocks from Ben Benson's Steakhouse to the New School for Social Research, you will remain the same person. But that is a rather limited view of reality.

RUSH. *(On air from prison.)* Coming to you live from Cellblock 8, this *is* the Rush Limbaugh Program. I was in the shower room this morning, bumped into a guy doing 7 to 12 for a check-kiting scheme. Now, see, see, when I say the words "check-kiting scheme," your mind no doubt conjures up, oh I don't know, some little guy pocketed a couple of dollars out of a Safeway payroll account. No, my friends, we are talking about rather larger potatoes than that: this is the gentleman who kited the entire Shearson Lehmann Retirement Fund.

And he said, "What are *you* in for?" And I said, "I'm in for loving not wisely but too well." And his jaw dropped and he said, "Limbaugh?" I said, "Yeah." He said, "Limbaugh, I was your biggest fan! Limbaugh, you — you slept with a feminist. You wore a quartz crystal. Limbaugh, you *betrayed* us!"

(Sighs; taps on table.) And I mean, I — I didn't want

to get into it with him right there — about snakes, shedding skins. How if you eat the same flavor of ice cream day after day, week after week — if you don't grow, you die. Did not want to — get into it.

And I realized that in some sense he was not in that shower. He was not feeling the water on his body. He had no word of thanks for that hot water; no sacrament. What is it that takes us *out* of the moment? *(Pause.)* I'll be right back to tell you. *(Fade to black.)*

END OF PLAY

PROPERTY LIST

Spoon (BARRY)
Drinking glass (BARRY)
Newspaper clipping (RUSH)
Ratings paper (BARRY)
Pear (DR. ALVIN VOLT)
Pocket knife (DR. ALVIN VOLT)
Newspaper (RUSH)
Script (RUSH)
Bells (J. NEIL RODRIQUEZ)
Quartz-crystal necklace* (NINA)
Faxes (BARRY)
Paper with computer data (BARRY)
Various papers to read and rattle on the air (RUSH)

* Optional.

SOUND EFFECTS

Telephone ring

TODAY'S HOTTEST NEW PLAYS

❑ **MOLLY SWEENEY by Brian Friel, Tony Award-Winning Author of *Dancing at Lughnasa*.** Told in the form of monologues by three related characters, *Molly Sweeney* is mellifluous, Irish storytelling at its dramatic best. Blind since birth, Molly recounts the effects of an eye operation that was intended to restore her sight but which has unexpected and tragic consequences. *"Brian Friel has been recognized as Ireland's greatest living playwright. Molly Sweeney confirms that Mr. Friel still writes like a dream. Rich with rapturous poetry and the music of rising and falling emotions...Rarely has Mr. Friel written with such intoxicating specificity about scents, colors and contours." - New York Times.* [2M, 1W]

❑ **SWINGING ON A STAR (The Johnny Burke Musical) by Michael Leeds. 1996 Tony Award Nominee for Best Musical.** The fabulous songs of Johnny Burke are perfectly represented here in a series of scenes jumping from a 1920s Chicago speakeasy to a World War II USO Show and on through the romantic high jinks of the Bob Hope/Bing Crosby "Road Movies." Musical numbers include such favorites as "Pennies from Heaven," "Misty," "Ain't It a Shame About Mame," "Like Someone in Love," and, of course, the Academy Award winning title song, "Swinging on a Star." *"A WINNER. YOU'LL HAVE A BALL!" - New York Post. "A dazzling, toe-tapping, finger-snapping delight!" - ABC Radio Network. "Johnny Burke wrote his songs with moonbeams!" - New York Times.* [3M, 4W]

❑ **THE MONOGAMIST by Christopher Kyle.** Infidelity and mid-life anxiety force a forty-something poet to reevaluate his 60s values in a late 80s world. *"THE BEST COMEDY OF THE SEASON. Trenchant, dark and jagged. Newcomer Christopher Kyle is a playwright whose social satire comes with a nasty, ripping edge - Molière by way of Joe Orton." - Variety. "By far the most stimulating playwright I've encountered in many a buffaloed moon." - New York Magazine. "Smart, funny, articulate and wisely touched with rue...the script radiates a bright, bold energy." - The Village Voice.* [2M, 3W]

❑ **DURANG/DURANG by Christopher Durang.** These cutting parodies of *The Glass Menagerie* and *A Lie of the Mind*, along with the other short plays in the collection, prove once and for all that Christopher Durang is our theater's unequivocal master of outrageous comedy. *"The fine art of parody has returned to theater in a production you can sink your teeth and mind into, while also laughing like an idiot." - New York Times. "If you need a break from serious drama, the place to go is Christopher Durang's silly, funny, over-the-top sketches." - TheatreWeek.* [3M, 4W, flexible casting]

TODAY'S HOTTEST NEW PLAPS

❑ **THREE VIEWINGS by Jeffrey Hatcher.** Three comic-dramatic monologues, set in a midwestern funeral parlor, interweave as they explore the ways we grieve, remember, and move on. *"Finally, what we have been waiting for: a new, true, idiosyncratic voice in the theater. And don't tell me you hate monologues; you can't hate them more than I do. But these are much more: windows into the deep of each speaker's fascinating, paradoxical, unique soul, and windows out into a gallery of surrounding people, into hilarious and horrific coincidences and conjunctions, into the whole dirty but irresistible business of living in this damnable but spellbinding place we presume to call the world." - New York Magazine.* [1M, 2W]

❑ **HAVING OUR SAY by Emily Mann.** The Delany Sisters' Bestselling Memoir is now one of Broadway's Best-Loved Plays! Having lived over one hundred years apiece, Bessie and Sadie Delany have plenty to say, and their story is not simply African-American history or women's history...it is our history as a nation. *"The most provocative and entertaining family play to reach Broadway in a long time." - New York Times. "Fascinating, marvelous, moving and forceful." - Associated Press.* [2W]

❑ **THE YOUNG MAN FROM ATLANTA Winner of the 1995 Pulitzer Prize. by Horton Foote.** An older couple attempts to recover from the suicide death of their only son, but the menacing truth of why he died, and what a certain Young Man from Atlanta had to do with it, keeps them from the peace they so desperately need. *"Foote ladles on character and period nuances with a density unparalleled in any living playwright." - NY Newsday.* [5M, 4W]

❑ **SIMPATICO by Sam Shepard.** Years ago, two men organized a horse racing scam. Now, years later, the plot backfires against the ringleader when his partner decides to come out of hiding. *"Mr. Shepard writing at his distinctive, savage best." - New York Times.* [3M, 3W]

❑ **MOONLIGHT by Harold Pinter.** The love-hate relationship between a dying man and his family is the subject of Harold Pinter's first full-length play since *Betrayal*. *"Pinter works the language as a master pianist works the keyboard." - New York Post.* [4M, 2W, 1G]

❑ **SYLVIA by A.R. Gurney.** This romantic comedy, the funniest to come along in years, tells the story of a twenty-two year old marriage on the rocks, and of Sylvia, the dog who turns it all around. *"A delicious and dizzy new comedy." - New York Times. "FETCHING! I hope it runs longer than Cats!" - New York Daily News.* [2M, 2W]

DRAMATISTS PLAY SERVICE, INC.
440 Park Avenue South, New York, New York 10016 212-683-8960 Fax 212-213-1539